ITALIAN

Colophon

© 2003 Rebo International b.v., Lisse, The Netherlands

www.rebo-publishers.com – info@rebo-publishers.com

This 2nd edition reprinted 2004

Original recipes and photographs: © R&R Publishing Pty. Ltd.

Design, editing, production and layout: Minkowsky Graphics, Enkhuzien, The Netherlands

Translation and adaptation: American Pie, London, UK and Sunnyvale, California, USA

ISBN 90 366 1472 4

ITALIAN

passion and perfection, secrets of the trattoria for
creative cooking

REBO
PUBLISHERS

Foreword

Nothing is complicated in Italian cuisine, provided you have the basic ingredients — olive oil, coarse sea salt, black pepper, basil, rosemary, and Parmesan cheese. With these basics, if you have the Italian touch, you can concoct a delicious meal. If you have not done so already, you will probably fall in love with the purity of the flavors. Try Lamb Shanks with Rosemary, or Saltimbocca of Swordfish Fillets with Tomato Salsa, for instance. Start with Antipasti with Balsamic Vinegar Dressing, followed by Ravioli with Smoked Salmon. Buon appetito!

Abbreviations

tbsp = tablespoon

tsp = teaspoon

g = gram

kg = kilogram

fl oz = fluid ounce

lb = pound

oz = ounce

ml = milliliter

l = liter

°C = degree Celsius

°F = degree Fahrenheit

Where three measurements are given, the first is the American liquid measure.

Method

1. Place the slices of coppa under a hot broiler and broil until crisp. Place spinach, coppa, pinenuts, and avocado in a bowl.

2. Combine the oil and balsamic vinegar, pour the dressing over the salad, and then toss through the pecorino shavings.

3. Season with salt and pepper and serve.

Baby Spinach with Toasted Pinenuts and Avocado Salad

Ingredients

2⅔oz/80g coppa, sliced

2 scant cups/7oz/220g baby spinach

2oz/60g pinenuts, toasted

1 avocado, sliced

¼ cup/2fl oz/60ml olive oil

2 tbsp/1fl oz/30ml balsamic vinegar

¼ cup//2 oz/60g pecorino shavings

sea salt

freshly ground black pepper

Serves **6**

Method

1. Broil ciabatta slices on both sides for 2-3 minutes.

2. Brush with olive oil, spread with sun-dried tomato paste.

   Top with bocconcini or mozzarella cheese slices and shredded basil leaves.

   Leave the basil leaves whole if preferred.

Bruschetta with Bocconcini and Basil

Ingredients

1 ciabatta loaf, sliced in ¾ in/2cm slices

¼ cup/2fl oz/60ml olive oil

⅓ cup/3½ fl oz/100ml sun-dried tomato paste

6oz/180g bocconcini or mozzarella cheese, each ball sliced into 5 slices

½ cup/2oz/60g basil leaves, sliced, or whole leaves

Method

1. Heat the oil in a saucepan, and sauté the onion and garlic for 5 minutes or until the onion is soft. Add the potatoes and cook for a further 5 minutes. Add the carrots, celery, and zucchini and cook for another 5 minutes.

2. Add the beef broth, tomatoes, and cheese crust, bring to the boil, simmer covered, for 1 hour. If the soup becomes too thick can add more broth.

3. Add the minced parsley and cannellini beans, and heat for a further 10 minutes.

4. To serve, remove the cheese crust, season with salt and black pepper, and serve with crusty bread.

Minestrone

Ingredients

5 tbsp/2½fl oz/85ml olive oil

1 medium brown onion, sliced

1 clove of garlic, crushed

1 cup/8oz/250g peeled and diced potatoes

⅔ cup/150g/5oz thinly sliced carrots

125g/4oz thinly sliced celery

⅔ cup/5oz/150g sliced zucchini (courgette)

1 quart/1¾ pints/1 l beef broth

1¾ cups/14oz/420g can Italian peeled tomatoes

rind from piece of Parmesan cheese

1 tbsp/15g minced parsley

1¾ cups/420g/14oz cannellini beans, canned

salt and freshly ground black pepper

Method

1. Heat the oil in a saucepan, add the garlic, onion, and rosemary, and cook on medium heat for 3-5 minutes, or until soft.

2. Add the tomato pesto and cook for 1 minute.

3. Add carrot, potato, and sweet potato, and cook a further 5 minutes. Add the chicken broth and pepper & salt, bring to boil, reduce the heat, and simmer, covered, for 30-40 minutes, or until vegetables are soft.

4. Purée the soup in a food processor (you may have to do this in two batches), return the soup to pan, add the rosemary, and heat through before serving. Add extra broth if soup is too thick.

Sweet Potato & Rosemary Soup

Ingredients

4 tbsp/40ml/1⅓fl oz olive oil

2 cloves of garlic, crushed

1 medium onion, chopped

1 tbsp/5g rosemary, chopped

2 tbsp/30ml tomato pesto

1 medium carrot, diced

1 large potato, diced

3 cups/1½lb/750g sweet potato, diced

1 quart/1¾ cups/1 l chicken broth

freshly ground pepper & salt

around 2 tbsp/30g rosemary, chopped

Method

1. Preheat the oven to 440°F/220°C.

2. Lightly oil a baking dish, place tomatoes in the dish, and bake 20 minutes, or until the skins have blistered. Set aside to cool, then peel and roughly chop.

3. Heat the oil in a saucepan, add the garlic and the onion, and cook for 5 minutes, or until soft. Add cumin and coriander, and cook for 1 minute, until well combined. Add tomatoes, bell peppers, and broth to the saucepan, bring to the boil, and simmer, (for 30 minutes. Add bread, balsamic vinegar and salt & pepper, and cook a further 5-10 minutes.

4. Serve with Parmesan cheese, if desired.

Roasted Tomato, Red Pepper, & Bread Soup

Ingredients

5 cups/2¼lb/1kg plum tomatoes, roasted

2 red bell peppers, roasted, roughly chopped

2½ tbsp/40ml olive oil

2 onions, minced

3 cloves of garlic, crushed

2 tsp/10g ground cumin

1 tsp/5g ground coriander

1 quart/1¾ pints/1 l chicken broth

2 slices white bread, crusts removed and torn into pieces

4 tsp/20ml balsamic vinegar

salt & freshly ground pepper, to taste

Method

1. Arrange tomatoes, bocconcini, and basil leaves on individual plates.

2. Drizzle with extra virgin olive oil and balsamic vinegar, and sprinkle with sea salt and freshly ground black pepper.

3. Serve with crusty bread.

Tomato, Bocconcini, and Basil Salad with Balsamic Dressing

Ingredients

1¾ oz/13oz/410g Roma tomatoes, sliced thickly

1 cup/8 oz/250g bocconcini, sliced

½ cup/2oz/50g fresh basil leaves, shredded

extra-virgin olive oil to taste

balsamic vinegar to taste

salt and freshly ground black pepper

crusty bread, for serving

Method

1. Lightly brush a broiler pan with oil, and heat. Broil the zucchini slices, 2-3 minutes each side, then remove and set aside.

2. Add the sausages and cook for 6-8 minutes, turning frequently, then remove from the broiler, and set aside to cool. Slice sausages into 1in/2½cm slices.

3. Brush slices of bread with oil, and cook under broiler for 2-3 minutes, each side. Combine arugula leaves, basil, sausages, zucchini, sun-dried tomatoes and Parmesan in a large bowl.

4. Mix together oil, lemon juice and salt & pepper, and whisk. Drizzle dressing over salad.

Italian Sausage with Zucchini and Arugula

Ingredients

4tsp/20ml olive oil

2 medium zucchini (courgettes), cut into 1cm/½in slices

350g/11oz Italian sausages (5-6 sausages)

1 thin French stick, cut in 1in/2cm slices

2½ tbsp/40ml extra-virgin olive oil

4oz/125g arugula (rocket) leaves, washed

¼ cup/2 tbsp basil leaves, shredded

125g/4oz semi sun-dried tomatoes

¼ cup/2 tbsp grated Parmesan

Dressing:

4 tbsp/60ml/2fl oz olive oil

2½ tbsp/40ml lemon juice

freshly ground pepper & salt

Method

1. Toast bread slices, for 2–3 minutes on each side.

2. Brush with a little olive oil, and spread a thin layer of roasted
   puréed garlic on each slice.

3. In a bowl, mix together tomatoes, onions, basil, vinegar, and olive oil,
   and season with salt and pepper.

4. Serve toasted bread with tomato mixture on top.

Bruschetta with Tomato and Basil

Ingredients

1 ciabatta loaf or French stick,

sliced into ¾in/2cm slices

olive oil, for brushing

2 cloves of garlic, roasted and puréed;

1¾ cups/440g/14oz plum tomatoes, diced

1 small red onion, minced

1 tbsp/15g basil, chopped

2 tbsp/50ml olive oil

1 tbsp/15ml balsamic vinegar

salt

black pepper, freshly ground

Method

1. Trim off the thick asparagus ends and cook asparagus in boiling water for 4 minutes, until tender, but still crisp. Rinse under cold water, until asparagus is cool, then dry with paper towels.

2. For the dressing: place the lemon juice in a bowl then gradually add oil, as for mayonnaise, whisking until dressing is thick. Season with salt and pepper.

3. Pour the dressing over asparagus, and serve with the pancetta and pecorino cheese shavings.

Ingredients

1lb/500g asparagus

8 thin slices of pancetta, cut into pieces

⅓ cup/3½ fl oz/100ml extra-virgin olive oil

1 lemon, juice squeezed

pecorino shavings

sea salt

freshly ground black pepper

Asparagus with Pecorino and Pancetta

Method

1. Preheat the oven to 350°F/180°C.

2. Combine the olive oil, lemon juice, lemon rind, garlic, pepper, and salt in a bowl. Set aside.

3. Heat the extra oil in a large pan, add the quail and the chopped sage leaves, and brown quickly. Set aside in a baking dish.

4. To the pan, add oil, the lemon juice-mixture and the chicken broth. Return to the heat, bring to the boil, and simmer for 1 minute (to reduce liquid), stirring with a wooden spoon.

5. Pour the pan juices over the quail and roast in the preheated oven for 20-25 minutes. Garnish with whole sage leaves.

Ingredients

5 tbsp/40ml olive oil

5 tsp/20ml lemon juice

½ tsp/2.5g grated lemon rind

1 clove of garlic, crushed

freshly ground pepper

sea salt

Butterflied Quail with Lemon & Sage Leaves

1 tbsp/15ml extra-virgin olive oil

4 quails, butterflied

1 bunch sage leaves, 1 tbsp/15g chopped,

the rest for garnish

¼ cup/2 fl oz/75ml chicken broth

Italian

Method

1. Preheat oven to 350°F/180°C.

2. Lightly butter an ovenproof dish, and arrange the potato slices in overlapping rows in the dish, seasoning with salt and pepper, garlic and nutmeg, in between each layer.

3. Mix the flour and Parmesan cheese into the cream, and pour over the potatoes. Sprinkle with extra Parmesan cheese, and bake in the oven for 40-45 minutes, or until potatoes are cooked.

4. To make the pesto, place the mint, parsley, garlic, pinenuts, and cheeses in the bowl of a food processor and process until finely chopped. Add the olive oil in a steady stream, with processor still running. Season with salt and pepper, and set aside.

5. Preheat broiler pan or griddle and grease lightly with a little oil. Season lamb with extra salt and pepper to taste. Broil the lamb on both sides or approximately 5-10 minutes or until done to your liking.

6. Serve the lamb, sliced diagonally, on a bed of creamy potatoes with the mint pesto.

Ingredients

1lb/500g potatoes, sliced thinly

salt and freshly ground pepper

1 clove of garlic, crushed

1 tsp/5g nutmeg

1 tbsp/15g all-purpose flour

⅓ cup/ Parmesan cheese, grated

1 cup/8 fl oz/250ml heavy cream

2 tbsp/20g Parmesan cheese, grated

salt & freshly ground black pepper

Chargrilled Lamb with Mint Pesto and Creamy Potatoes

Mint Pesto:

1 cup/4oz/125g mint leaves

½ cup/2½ oz/75g parsley leaves

2 cloves of garlic

½ cup/4pz/125g pinenuts, toasted

3 tbsp/45g Parmesan cheese, grated

3 tbsp/45g pecorino cheese, grated

⅓ cup/3½ fl oz/100ml olive oil

4 (1lb/450g) lamb shanks, boned

salt & freshly ground black pepper

Italian

Method

1. Preheat the oven to 400°F/200°C.

2. Combine ricotta, rocket, pinenuts, bell pepper, and pepper & salt in a small bowl, and mix together, until smooth.

3. Place 1-2 tbsp of ricotta mixture under the skin of each chicken breast. Lightly grease a baking dish. Place chicken breasts in the dish, sprinkle with pepper and salt, place 1 tsp/5g butter on each breast, pour broth around the chicken, bake, for 20-25 minutes.

4. Serve chicken with pan-juices and an arugula (rocket) salad.

Chicken with Ricotta, Arugula, & Roasted Red Bell Pepper

Ingredients

220g/7oz fresh ricotta

1 cup/4oz/125g arugula (rocket), chopped

¼ cup/2oz/50g pinenuts, toasted

½ red bell pepper, roasted and finely chopped

freshly ground pepper & salt

4 x /6-7oz/185-220g

chicken breasts, with skin

4 tsp butter

1 cup/8fl oz/250ml chicken broth

Method

1. Combine the flour, pepper, and salt in a bowl and coat the chicken evenly with the flour, shaking off the excess.

2. Heat oil and butter in a frying pan, add the chicken, and cook, over medium heat, for 5-6 minutes each side. Remove from the pan and keep warm.

3. To make the basil cream sauce, wipe out the frying pan, heat the butter, add the garlic, and cook for 2 minutes. Add chicken broth, cream, and lemon juice, bring to boil, and reduce a little.

4. Just before serving, add the basil season with pepper and salt, and serve the sauce with the chicken.

Ingredients

4 x 7 oz/220g chicken breasts

3 tbsp/45g all-purpose flour

freshly ground pepper and salt

1 tbsp/15ml olive oil

1 tbsp/15g butter

Basil Cream Sauce:

1 tbsp/15g butter

Chicken with Basil Cream Sauce

2 cloves of garlic, crushed

½ cup/4fl oz/125ml chicken broth

½ cup/4fl oz/125ml cup cream

2fl oz/60ml lemon juice

2 tbsp/30g basil, finely chopped

freshly ground pepper

sea salt

Italian

Method

1. Preheat the oven to 300°F/150°C.

2. Heat a broiler pan and brush lightly with oil. Brush eggplant slices with oil and broil for 2-3 minutes each side. Place bell pepper under a hot broiler, and cook, until skin is black.

3. Brush tomato slices with oil, sprinkle with pepper, place on a lightly oiled baking-tray, and roast in a slow oven for 20-30 minutes.

4. On a serving platter, place 2 slices of eggplant, top with 3 strips of bell pepper, 3 slices tomato, 3 slices bocconcini or mozzarella, and 2 strips red bell pepper. Garnish with basil leaves.

5. Combine the dressing ingredients. Drizzle balsamic dressing over dish, and sprinkle with a good grinding of sea salt and black pepper just before serving. Serve with crusty Italian bread.

Ingredients

¼ cup/2fl oz/50ml olive oil

2 large eggplant (aubergines), around 11oz/350g each,

sliced into 8 slices each ½ - ¾ in/1-1½cm thick

1 red bell pepper, quartered, seeded, roasted, and thinly sliced

4 beefsteak tomatoes, sliced into 1cm/½ in slices, and roasted

freshly ground black pepper

Eggplant, Bell Pepper, Tomato &
Bocconcini with Balsamic Dressing

bocconcini or mozzarella, sliced; 3 slices per serving

basil leaves, to garnish

crusty Italian bread, for serving

Balsamic dressing:

2fl oz/60ml olive oil

2 tbsp/30ml balsamic vinegar

sea salt & freshly ground black pepper

Italian

33

Method

1. Place quail eggs in a small saucepan of cold water,
    bring to the boil, and boil for 3 minutes. Rinse under cold water,
    until eggs are cool, then peel and cut in half.

2. Combine the beans, prosciutto, quail eggs, and Parmesan
    cheese in a bowl. Sprinkle with the black pepper and sea salt.
    Drizzle dressing over the dish, and serve.

Ingredients

6 quail eggs

1 cup/8 oz/250g baby green beans, blanched

6 thin slices prosciutto, cut into strips

Parmesan cheese, shaved

freshly ground black pepper

sea salt

Green Beans with Prosciutto, Parmesan, Extra Virgin Olive Oil & Vinegar

Dressing:

2 tbsp/30ml extra-virgin olive oil

1 tbsp/15ml white wine vinegar

Italian

Method

1. Combine the garlic, olive oil, and lemon juice in a dish, and marinate the fish steaks for 1 hour.

2. Grease a broiler pan and broil fish for 3 minutes on each side.

3. Serve with Basil Aioli and Parmesan Potatoes.

Basil Aioli

1. In a food processor, place basil, 1 tbsp/15ml oil, garlic, egg yolks, lemon juice. Process until smooth.

2. With processor running, add oil in a thin stream and beat until thick. Add water, if liked, to make a thinner aioli.

3. Add salt & pepper, to taste.

Parmesan Potatoes

1. Place potatoes in a saucepan with salted water, and cook until potatoes are almost cooked, but still a little hard in the center. Drain.

2. Heat the oil and butter in a pan, add potatoes, and cook until brown. Add cheese, and cook, until potatoes are crisp.

Cod with Basil Aioli

Ingredients

1 clove of garlic, minced

2 tbsp/50ml olive oil

1 tbsp/15ml lemon juice

4 cod steaks

½ cup/2oz/60g fresh basil leaves, chopped

1 quantity of Parmesan Potatoes

3 tsp/75ml lemon juice

1 tbsp/15ml water

pepper, freshly ground

salt, to taste

Basil Aioli

1 cup/4oz/125g basil leaves

½ cup/4fl oz/125ml olive oil

1 clove of garlic, minced

2 egg yolks

Parmesan Potatoes

400g/13oz potatoes, peeled and cubed

1 tbsp/15ml olive oil

1 tbsp/15g butter

1 tbsp/15g grated Parmesan

Method

1. Preheat oven to 350°F/180°C.

2. Heat the oil in a large pan, add garlic and lamb cutlets, and brown on medium heat for 2-3 minutes on each side.

3. Add wine and cook for 2 minutes. Mix the tomato paste with the beef broth and add to the lamb cutlets. Add the rosemary, black olives, and pepper.

4. Transfer lamb to a casserole dish and bake, for 30-40 minutes.

Ingredients

1 tbsp/15ml olive oil

2 cloves of garlic, minced

8-12 lamb cutlets, depending on size

⅔ cup/5fl oz/150ml white wine

Lamb Cutlets with Olives & Rosemary

⅔ cup/5fl oz/150ml beef broth

2 tbsp/30ml tomato paste

2 sprigs rosemary, coarsely chopped

⅓ cup/2½ oz/100g black olives

freshly ground black pepper

Italian

Method

1. Heat 1 tbsp/15ml oil in a large heavy-based saucepan, add root vegetables, and cook quickly, until brown.
Set aside on a plate. Add the rest of the oil to the pan, and brown the garlic and shanks for a few minutes.

2. To the pan, add the broth, water, red wine, tomato paste, rosemary, bouquet garni, and pepper & salt. Bring to the boil, reduce the heat, and leave to simmer, with the lid on for 20 minutes.

3. Return the vegetables to the pan, and continue to cook for another 30 minutes, until vegetables and lamb are cooked.

4. Before serving, remove the bouquet garni and check the seasoning.

Ingredients

4 tbsp/60ml olive oil

2 parsnips, peeled, and cut into large chunks

1 medium sweet potato, peeled, and cut into large chunks

1 swede, peeled, and cut into large chunks

1 bunch spring onions, trimmed

2½ tbsp/40ml olive oil, extra

2 cloves of garlic, crushed

Lamb Shanks with Root Vegetables

4 lamb shanks

7fl oz/200ml beef broth

2fl oz-60ml water

4fl oz-125ml red wine

1 tbsp/15g tomato paste

2 sprigs rosemary, chopped

bouquet garni

freshly ground pepper & salt

Italian

Method

1. Preheat the oven to 350°F/180°C.

2. Place lamb on a board, skin side down. Brush inside with oil, and sprinkle with garlic.

3. Add half the sun-dried tomatoes, place 2 sprigs of rosemary inside each loin of lamb. Season with pepper and salt.

4. Truss lamb up with kitchen twine, place on a roasting rack, roast for 30 minutes, or until lamb is done to your liking. Leave to rest for 10 minutes, covered.

5. Rosemary jus: in a small saucepan, place broth, vinegar, sugar, and rosemary. Bring to the boil, leave to simmer, and reduce, for 5 minutes.

6. Serve sliced lamb with rosemary jus.

Ingredients

2 lamb loins each weighing 375-410g/12-13oz

2½ tbsp/40ml olive oil

1 clove of garlic (crushed)

⅔ cup/5oz/155g semi sun-dried tomatoes, sliced

4 sprigs rosemary

freshly ground pepper & salt

kitchen twine, for trussing lamb

Loin of Lamb with Rosemary, Garlic & Sun-dried Tomatoes

Rosemary Jus:

1 cup/250ml/8fl oz beef broth

2 tsp/10ml balsamic vinegar

2 tsp/10g sugar

1 tbsp/15g rosemary, chopped

Method

1. In a shallow bowl, combine flour, herbs, pepper, and salt.

2. Coat sardine fillets with flour mixture, pressing mixture firmly onto fish.

3. Heat oil in a large frying pan. Add sardines 4 at a time, and cook for 1–2 minutes each side, or until crisp and lightly browned.

4. Serve with lemon wedges and a mixed leaf salad.

Pan-fried Sardines with Mixed Herbs

Ingredients

⅓ cup/3½ oz/100g all-purpose flour

3 tbsp mixed fresh herbs (parsley, basil, oregano, and marjoram), roughly chopped

½ tsp/2.5g coarse black pepper

pinch sea salt

3lb/1.5kg sardine fillets

2fl oz/60ml olive oil

2 lemons, cut into wedges

Method

1. Place red kidney beans and cannellini beans in a bowl.

   Cover with cold water and set aside to soak overnight. Drain.

2. Heat oil in a saucepan over a medium heat, add bacon,

   onion, and garlic and cook, stirring, for 5 minutes or until onion

   is tender. Add celery, carrots, and potatoes and cook

   for 1 minute longer.

3. Stir in broth, tomatoes, cabbage, pasta or rice, red kidney beans,

   cannellini beans, herbs, and black pepper to taste and bring to

   the boil. Cook at a rolling boil for 10 minutes, then reduce heat

   and simmer, stirring occasionally, for 1 hour, or until beans are

   tender.

   Sprinkle with Parmesan cheese and serve.

Note:

Extra vegetables of your choice may be added—this is a good way
to use up vegetable leftovers.

Ingredients

⅓ cup/3oz/90g dried red kidney beans

⅓ cup/3oz/90g dried cannellini beans

2 tbsp/60ml olive oil

2oz/60g cooked bacon, chopped

1 onion, minced

1 clove of garlic, crushed

3 stalks celery, sliced

2 carrots, diced

2 potatoes, diced

6 cups/2½ cups/1½ l chicken or vegetable broth

Mixed **Bean Soup**

1 ¾ cups/14oz/440g canned tomatoes,

undrained and mashed

¼ cabbage, finely shredded

¼ cup/2oz/60g small pasta shapes or rice

1 tsp/5g dried mixed herbs

freshly ground black pepper

grated Parmesan cheese, to taste

Italian

Method

1. Heat the butter and oil in a pan, add the garlic, and cook,
    for 2 minutes. Add the mushrooms and cook for 1-2 minutes
    on each side.

2. Add the lemon juice, cream, chives and salt & pepper,
    and cook for 1 minute, until combined.

3. Serve with polenta.

Ingredients

2 tbsp/50g butter

2 tbsp/50ml olive oil

2 cloves of garlic, minced

4 cups/1lb/500g flat portobello mushrooms,

sliced ¾in/1.5cm thick

2 tbsp/50ml lemon juice

½ cup/4fl oz/125ml heavy cream

2 tbsp/50g chives, finely sliced

salt & freshly ground pepper

1 cup/250g/8oz cooked polenta

Mushrooms with Lemon Cream Sauce

Italian

Method

1. Cook pasta in boiling salted water until just cooked (al dente). Drain and set aside.

2. Heat oil in a saucepan, add garlic and pancetta, cook for 2 minutes, or until garlic is soft and flavors are well combined.

3. Add the pasta, tomato sauce, semi sun-dried tomatoes, rocket, and salt and freshly ground pepper to the pan, and heat through.

4. Serve with shavings of Parmesan cheese.

Ingredients

1lb/500g paesani or penne pasta

1 tbsp/15ml extra-virgin olive oil

2 cloves of garlic, crushed

3oz/100g hot pancetta, coarsely chopped

⅓ cup/2½oz/100g semi sun-dried tomatoes

1 cup/8fl oz/250 ml Italian tomato sauce

1 bunch rocket (about 1 cup/4oz/125g),
washed and drained

salt & freshly ground pepper

Parmesan cheese shavings

Paesani with Rocket,
Hot Pancetta & Sun-dried Tomatoes

Italian

Method

1. To make the pizza dough, combine water, yeast and sugar in a bowl, add 4 scant cups/13oz/400g of the flour, and stir, until mixture is a liquid paste.

2. Gradually add another 4 cups/1 lb/500g flour, then the oil and salt, and work together with your hands until the mixture forms an elastic ball of dough. Knead the bread with your hands for 10 minutes, until mixture is very elastic and smooth. (Alternatively, you can use an electric mixer with a dough hook, and knead on a low speed for 10 minutes.)

3. Take a piece of dough and roll it into a ball the size of an orange. Place on a floured tray and repeat, until all the dough is used up. Cover tray with a damp cloth and leave in a warm place for 2 hours, or until dough has risen.

4. Preheat the oven to 475°F/250°C.

5. Dust a cookie sheet and the work surface with flour. Divide the dough into eight or ten pieces. Take one piece of dough, and press it out with your hands to form a thick disk.

6. Roll out the dough in one direction, turn 90°, and roll again in another direction, repeating this process until dough forms a 3in/8cm-diameter circle. Repeat with the rest of the pieces of dough.

Ingredients

1 quantity of pizza dough

50ml/1⅔fl oz chili oil

4 potatoes, thinly sliced

2 small red onions, thinly sliced

3 sprigs rosemary, chopped

Pizza dough

500ml/16 fl oz warm water

1 package dry yeast

1 tsp/5g superfine (caster) sugar

9 cups/1kg/2½ lb all-purpose (strong plain flour)

1 tbsp/15ml extra-virgin olive oil

2 tsp/10g sea salt

Chili Oil

60ml/2fl oz extra-virgin olive oil

2 red chili peppers, seeded and finely chopped

1 clove of garlic, crushed

2 sprigs rosemary, chopped

black pepper, freshly ground

sea salt

Potato & Spanish Onion Pizza with Chili Oil

4. Place on a baking tray and brush with the chili oil (see below). Top with potato, onion. and rosemary, and bake for 5-10 minutes, or until brown. Top with rocket before serving, and drizzle with a little oil.

Note: Variations of toppings can be used: Rocket & parmesan; sun-dried tomatoes, Bocconcini and basil.

Chili oil

1. In a small saucepan, heat oil over low heat, turn off heat, add chili and garlic. Leave for 10 minutes to allow the flavors to infuse through the oil.

2. Add the rosemary, pepper, and salt, and leave to cool.

3. Store in airtight container.

Makes about ⅓ cup/3½fl oz/ 100ml

Italian

53

Method

1. Place lamb shanks on a board, and make cuts in the edges, to stop the meat from curling up. Heat the oil in a large frying pan.

2. Coat the shanks with seasoned flour and brown quickly in pan, for 2-3 minutes each side. Remove from the pan and keep warm.

3. Add the garlic, onion, carrot, and celery to the pan and cook for 5-8 minutes, or until soft. Add wine, and cook, until evaporated. Add the tomatoes and the stock, and return the shanks to the pan.

4. Bring to the boil, and add the herbs and salt & pepper. Reduce the heat, then cover and simmer for 1-1½ hours, or until the meat starts to come away from the bone.

Osso Bucco

Ingredients

1kg/2lb veal shanks

1-2 tbsp/25-50g all-purpose flour, seasoned

2 tbsp/30ml olive oil

1 clove of garlic, minced

1 onion, minced

1 carrot, finely diced

2 celery stalks, finely diced

½ cup/4fl oz/125ml white wine

4 plum tomatoes, peeled and chopped

1 cup/8fl oz/250ml beef stock

2 tbsp/30ml tomato paste

1 tbsp/15g basil, finely chopped

1 tbsp/15g parsley, finely chopped

salt & pepper, to taste

Method

1. Preheat the broiler.

2. Heat the butter in a pan, add the veal, and cook for 2-3 minutes on each side. Remove from the heat.

3. Place 2 slices of cheese on top of each piece of veal, and place under a hot broiler for 2-3 minutes, or until cheese has melted. Cut each veal piece in half, and top each half place with a slice of eggplant and 2 tomato halves. Repeat the layering for the other pieces of veal.

4. Heat the remaining pan juices, add chicken broth and basil, bring to the boil, and then simmer for 2 minutes.

5. To serve, pour the pan juices over the veal, and serve immediately.

Veal Scallopini with Mozzarella, Eggplant & Roasted Tomatoes

Ingredients

2 tbsp/2 oz/30g butter

4 veal scallops, 3-5oz/90-155g, pounded

1 scant cup/7 oz/200g mozzarella cheese,

cut into ⅛ in/½ cm thick slices

2 medium eggplant (aubergine) sliced into

½cm/¼in slices, broiled

2½ tbsp/40ml olive oil

8 beefsteak tomatoes, halved and roasted

250ml/8fl oz chicken broth

1 tbsp/15g chopped fresh basil

Method

1. Preheat the oven to 350°F/180°C.

2. Boil the potatoes, until soft. Drain, then mash, or purée, and add the olive oil, chopped capers and 1 tbsp/15g of the roasted garlic. Mix well, season with salt and pepper, to taste, and set aside until ready to serve.

3. Heat 2 tbsp/30ml olive oil in a pan, and brown the veal on both sides, until well sealed. This will take approximately 5 minutes. Remove the veal from the pan, and place on a rack in a baking dish. Rub veal with 1 tbsp/15g of roasted garlic and 1 tbsp/15g of thyme leaves, season with salt and pepper, and add half the wine and broth to the baking dish.

4. Roast in the oven for 20 minutes, or until veal is cooked to your liking. Wrap in foil and let rest for 10 minutes.

5. Add remaining broth, wine and thyme to the pan-juices and cook over a medium heat for 5 minutes, until the liquid has reduced by a third.

6. Serve veal on a bed of mashed potatoes with pan juices and sage leaves.

Ingredients

1½lb/750g potatoes, peeled, chopped

½ cup/4fl oz/125ml olive oil

1 tbsp/15g capers, chopped

2 tbsp/30g roasted garlic purée

salt

Rack of Veal with Thyme on Roasted Garlic Mashed Potato

freshly ground black pepper

2 tbsp olive oil

1kg/2lb (8 points) rack of veal

2 tbsp thyme leaves

300ml/10fl oz white wine

300ml/10fl oz chicken broth

Italian

Method

1. Cook the pasta in boiling salted water until just cooked (al dente). Drain, and rinse in cold water.

2. Heat 2 tbsp of the oil in a pan, add the garlic and chili peppers, and cook for 2-3 minutes. Return the cooked pasta to the pan, add the remaining ingredients, and heat through.

3. Serve immediately with Parmesan cheese.

Penne with Tuna, Olives & Artichokes

Ingredients

500g/1lb penne pasta

6 tbsp olive oil

2 cloves of garlic, minced

3 chili peppers, seeded and finely chopped

1 cup black olives, seeded

410g/13oz can artichokes

2 tbsp capers, chopped finely

440g/14oz can tuna, drained

Method

1. In a small saucepan, combine the orange juice, sugar, butter, cream and Triple Sec. Heat, until butter has melted and bring to the boil.

2. Reduce the heat, and simmer, until sauce thickens.

3. Heat oil in a large frying pan. Place all ingredients for fritters in a large mixing-bowl, and mix together, until well combined.

4. Place 1 tbsp of mixture in a sauté pan, and cook 3-4 at a time, for 1-2 minutes, turning over to cook on both sides. Take out with a slotted spoon, and drain on absorbent paper.

5. To serve the fritters, dust with icing sugar, serve with orange sauce. Garnish with orange segments.

Ingredients

Sauce:

250m/8fl oz orange juice, strained

⅓ cup caster sugar

2 tbsp butter

40ml/1⅓oz cream

1 tbsp Triple Sec or Cointreau

Ricotta Fritters with Orange Sauce

Fritters:

1 cup oil, for frying

250g/8oz fresh ricotta, pulped

¼ cup flour, sifted

40g/1⅓oz caster sugar

2 eggs

1 tbsp orange zest

For Serving:

2 tbsp powdered sugar

1 orange, segmented

Italian

Method

1. Place broth in a saucepan and bring to the boil.

   Leave simmering.

2. Heat oil in a large saucepan, add garlic and onion, and cook

   for 5 minutes, or until soft. Add rice, and stir, until well coated.

3. Pour in wine, and cook, until the liquid has been absorbed.

   Add the broth, a ladle at a time, stirring continuously, until liquid

   has been absorbed, before adding the next ladle of broth.

   Keep adding broth this way, and stirring, until all the broth

   is used, and until the rice is cooked, but still a little firm to bite.

4. Add the spinach, cheese and seasonings, stir, and cook, until

   spinach is just wilted and cheese has melted.

5. Serve immediately.

Ingredients

1 quart/1¾ pints/1 l chicken broth

2 tbsp olive oil

2 cloves of garlic, crushed

1 onion, finely chopped

2 cups/1 lb/450g Arborio (short-grain) rice

½ cup/125ml/4fl oz white wine

Risotto with Baby Spinach & Gorgonzola

2 scant cups/220g/7oz baby spinach

2 scant cups/220g/7oz Gorgonzola cheese,

in small pieces

salt & freshly ground pepper

Method

1. Heat 2 tbsp/2 fl oz/60ml the oil in a pan, add the garlic, and cook over a medium heat, until the garlic is slightly browned and golden.

2. Reduce the heat, and add tomatoes, basil, salt and pepper, and cook for 5 minutes (or until tomatoes are just heated through).

3. Cook cappellini pasta in boiling salted water, until al dente. Add remaining oil.

4. Serve with tomato mixture over cappellini pasta.

Cappellini with Tomatoes, Garlic, and Basil

Ingredients

½ cup/125ml/4fl oz olive oil

6 cloves of garlic, thinly sliced

2 cups/550g/18oz beefsteak tomatoes,

seeded and diced

⅓ cup/2 oz/55g basil, shredded

salt

freshly ground black pepper

13oz/410g cappellini

Method

1. Preheat oven to 440°F/220°C.

2. Place pumpkin, potato, sweet potato, oil, half the rosemary and sea salt in a baking dish, mix together, and bake for 20 minutes, or until just cooked.

3. Grease, and line with paper, a 12-cup muffin pan.

4. In a bowl, mix together the eggs, cream, milk, garlic, cheese, rosemary and the salt & pepper. Add potato, pumpkin, and sweet potato.

5. Pour into muffin pans and bake (at 350°F/180°C) for 30-35 minutes.

Ingredients

300g/10oz butternut pumpkin, peeled, seeded and diced into 2cm/¾in pieces

220g/7oz potatoes, peeled and diced into 2cm/¾in pieces

220g/7oz sweet potatoes, peeled and diced into 2cm/¾in pieces

1 tbsp olive oil

Roast Pumpkin, Potato & Rosemary Frittata

2 sprigs rosemary, roughly chopped

½ tsp sea salt

4 eggs

½ cup cream

½ cup milk

1 clove of garlic, minced

½ cup Parmesan cheese, grated

salt & pepper, to taste

Italian

Method

1. Combine oil, lemon juice and pepper in a large ceramic dish.

    Add salmon cutlets and leave to marinate for 3-4 hours.

    Proceed to make the Dill Hollandaise Sauce.

    Steps 2, 3, 4, resume preparation of salmon at step 5.

2. Dill hollandaise sauce: In a small saucepan add vinegar,

    pepper and water. Bring to the boil, then reduce, until

    1 tbsp of the liquid is left.

3. Place egg yolks and vinegar mixture in a food processor, and

    process, for 1 minute. With the motor still running, gradually

    add the hot melted butter, and process, until thick.

4. Add lemon juice, dill, and salt & pepper, to taste,

    and keep warm.

5. Lightly oil and heat a broiler pan, or preheat a grill.

    Cook salmon cutlets for 2-3 minutes each side, until done

    to your liking.

    Note: Grill may take a little longer.

6. Serve salmon with Dill hollandaise sauce dribbled over

7. Trim asparagus, and blanch in a bowl of boiling water,

    for 2-3 minutes.

8. Serve fish with asparagus and hollandaise sauce on the side.

Ingredients

40ml/1⅓fl oz extra-virgin olive oil

1 tbsp lemon juice

¼ tsp coarse black pepper

4 salmon cutlets, each 220g/7oz extra oil,

for broiler

1 bunch asparagus, for serving

Salmon Cutlets with Dill Hollandaise Sauce

Dill Hollandaise Sauce:

85ml/2½fl oz white wine vinegar

freshly ground pepper

60ml/2fl oz water

4 egg yolks

220g/7oz unsalted butter, melted

40ml/1⅓fl oz lemon juice

3 tbsp fresh dill, chopped

extra freshly ground pepper & salt

Italian

Method

1. Using a steak hammer, pound the veal until thin.

2. Heat the butter in a pan, add the veal, and brown quickly,
    on both sides. Remove from pan, top each with 2 slices
    mozzarella, 2 slices prosciutto and 2-3 sage leaves.
    Secure together with toothpicks.

3. Under a hot broiler, broil veal for approximately 2 minutes,
    until cheese has just started to melt. Reheat butter, add the sage
    and cook for 1 minute. Add the white wine and reduce the
    sauce slightly.

4. Pour the sauce over the veal, and serve immediately.

Ingredients

4 veal scallops each 4oz/125g

2-3 tbsp/50-75g butter

1 scant cup/220g/7oz mozzarella, sliced into 8 rounds

8 slices prosciutto

1 bunch sage (around 4oz/125g)

Veal Saltimbocca

2 tsp sage, roughly chopped

½ cup white wine

¼ cup chicken broth

Italian

Method

1. Combine the marinade ingredients.

2. Place spatchcocked chicken in a large dish, pour the marinade over the birds, and place in refrigerator for 3-4 hours.

3. Preheat the oven to 350°F/180°C.

4. Place spatchcocks on a roasting rack, and roast in oven for 35-40 minutes, basting every 15 minutes, until cooked. Serve with Rosemary Potatoes.

Cornish Hens with Rosemary, Extra Virgin Olive Oil, & Lemon Juice

Ingredients

2 x 1lb/500g cornish hens (poussins), cut in half, backbone removed and flattened (spatchcocked)

Marinade:

¼ cup/2fl oz/60ml extra-virgin olive oil

2 tbsp/30ml lemon juice

1 tbsp/15g rosemary, roughly chopped

1 clove of garlic, crushed

freshly ground black pepper

Method

1. Soak the porcini mushrooms in boiling water for 20 minutes. Drain and chop. Set aside.

2. Heat the oil in a sauté pan, and cook the beef for a few minutes on each side. Remove from pan. Sauté the onion and garlic, for a few minutes. Combined the chopped porcini with the sliced shiitake and button mushrooms. Cook over high heat, until they are soft.

3. Add the wine and broth, bring to boil, and then simmer, for 10 minutes. Remove from the heat, add parsley, and season with salt and pepper.

4. Serve the beef with mushrooms and polenta, and sprinkle with extra minced parsley.

Ingredients

¼ cup/2 oz/50g porcini (cep) mushrooms, dried

¼ cup/2fl oz/60ml olive oil

2½lb/1 kg rump or fillet steak, cut into 6 slices

1 brown onion, minced

2 cloves of garlic, crushed

⅔ cup/5oz/150g fresh shiitake, sliced

⅔ cup/5oz/150g button mushrooms, sliced

Seared Beef with Mushrooms, Garlic, and Basil Polenta

4 tbsp/2fl oz/60ml red wine

1 cup/8fl oz/250ml brown broth

2 tbsp/30g parsley, minced

salt and pepper

extra parsley for garnish

2 cups/1 lb/500g basil and garlic polenta

Italian

77

Method

1. Combine the flour, pepper and salt in a shallow bowl, and coat the fish fillets evenly with flour, shaking off excess.

2. Heat the oil in a frying pan, add the fish, and cook over a medium heat for 5-6 minutes on each side, depending on thickness of fish. Set fish aside on a plate, and keep warm.

3. Wipe the pan, then add the butter. When it has melted, add garlic, and cook for 2 minutes. Add white wine and simmer, until the sauce reduces.

4. Just before serving, add chopped parsley to the sauce and serve with the fish.

Ingredients

½ cup/3 oz/75g all-purpose flour

1 tsp/15g coarse ground pepper

¼ tsp/1/25g sea salt

4 snapper fillets, each 7oz/220g/

2 tbsp/30ml olive oil

60g/2oz butter

2 cloves of garlic, (crushed)

½ cup/4fl oz/125ml white wine

2 tbsp/30 g minced parsley

Snapper Fillets with White Wine & Parsley

Method

1. Cook the spaghettini in boiling water with a little oil until al dente. Rinse under cold water, and set aside.

2. Heat half the oil and cook the garlic on a low heat, until beginning to turn color. Add the chili and tomato, and cook for a few minutes.

3. Add the clams, parsley, lemon juice, remaining oil, spaghettini, and a little of the water used to cook the clams, and heat through, for a further 5 minutes. Season with salt and black ground pepper.

4. Note: If using fresh clams, wash under running water, scraping the shells with a sharp knife or scourer. Put them in a large pan with a little water over a gentle heat, until they open. Discard any that do not open.

Ingredients

13oz/410g spaghettini

⅓ cup/2½ fl oz/85ml olive oil

4 cloves of garlic, sliced

4 red chili peppers, finely chopped

2 cups1 lb/450g canned tomatoes, finely diced

2¾ cups21oz/650g/ canned baby clams, or fresh if available

⅓ cup/2½ oz/75g minced parsley

2 lemons, juice squeezed

salt & freshly ground black pepper

Spaghettini with Baby Clams, Chili, and Garlic

Tip

If you use fresh littlneck or quahog clams on the shell, scrape
the shells with a sharp knife and sponge them.
Put them in a large pan with a little water and cook
on low heat until the shells open. Throw away any shells that
do not open.

Method

1. Place the salmon, 1 tbsp of egg white, cream, and dill in a food processor, and process, until well combined like a mousse.

2. Sprinkle the cornstarch on a work surface and lay wonton skins in rows of four.

3. Brush round the edge of every second skin with egg white. On alternate skins, place 1 tsp/5g of mixture in the center. Place the other skin on top, gently pinch the skins around mixture, to make ravioli pillows.

4. Half-fill a large saucepan with water and oil, bring to the boil, add 2-3 cups/8-12 oz/125-250g ravioli, cook, for 2-3 minutes. Set aside, and cover with plastic wrap.

5. For the lemon dill sauce: melt the butter in a saucepan, add the flour, and cook, for 1 minute). Add the wine, stir, until smooth, and then add the cream and lemon juice. Bring to the boil, and reduce, until sauce is a pouring consistency.

6. **To serve:** add the dill, and salt & pepper to the sauce, and pour it over the ravioli.

Smoked Salmon Ravioli with Lemon Dill Sauce

Ingredients

4oz/125g smoked salmon pieces

1 egg white

1½ tbsp/20ml heavy cream

2 tsp/10g fresh dill, coarsely chopped

2-3 tbsp/30-45g cornstarch

32 wonton skins

1 tsp/5ml oil

2-3 cups/ ravioli

Lemon Dill Sauce:

1 tbsp/½ oz/7g butter

1 tbsp/15g flour

¾ cup/6 fl oz white wine

¾ cup/6 fl oz thickened cream

½ lemon, juice squeezed

2 tbsp/30g dill, roughly chopped

salt & freshly ground pepper

Method

1. Melt butter in a large frying pan and cook mushrooms, green onions (scallions) and garlic for 4-5 minutes. Remove from pan and set aside. Add scallops to pan and cook for 2-3 minutes or until tender. Remove from pan and set aside.

2. Stir in wine, chili pepper, and parsley and cook over a high heat until reduced by half. Return mushroom mixture and scallops to pan, toss to combine.

Ingredients

3 tbsp/1½oz/45g butter

1 lb/500g button mushrooms

6 green onions (scallions), chopped

2 cloves of garlic, crushed

500g/1 lb scallops, cleaned

60ml/2fl oz dry white wine

1 red chili pepper, seeded and finely sliced

3 tbsp/45g minced parsley

Spicy Scallops and Mushrooms

Italian

Method

1. Combine basil pesto and olive oil.

2. Brush fish with pesto and set aside.

3. Heat broiler and cook fish, 2-3 minutes each side.

4. Combine all salsa ingredients in a small bowl, and mix well.

5. Serve the fish coated with salsa.

Method

1. Place the basil, pinenuts, garlic, and cheeses in a food processor, and grind into a paste.

2. With the motor still running, add oil in a steady stream, until well combined.

3. Season with salt and pepper, to taste.

4. Refrigerate, covered with a little olive oil, to prevent basil going brown.

Note: Pesto can be frozen.

Salsa:

2 beefsteak tomatoes, finely chopped

1 small red onion, minced

1 tsp/5g coarse black pepper

2 tbsp/30g chopped basil

40ml/1½fl oz extra-virgin olive oil

4 tsp/20ml lemon juice

Ingredients

4 tbsp/2oz/60ml basil pesto

4 tsp/20ml olive oil

4 swordfish steaks, each 6-7oz/185-220g

extra oil, for the broiler

Swordfish Steaks with Tomato Salsa

Pesto sauce:

1½ cups/6 oz/175g basil leaves

¼ cup/2 oz/60g pinenuts, toasted

2 cloves of garlic, roughly chopped

¼ cup/2 oz/50g Parmesan cheese, grated

¼ cup/2 oz/50g pecorino cheese, grated

5 tbsp/2½ fl oz/80ml olive oil

salt & freshly ground black pepper

Italian

Method

1. In a pan, heat the butter, add the mushrooms, and cook, for a few minutes. Remove from the heat and set aside.

2. Heat the oil in a large heavy-based saucepan, add the garlic and leek, and cook for 5-6 minutes, until cooked. Meanwhile, place broth in a saucepan and simmer gently.

3. Add the rice and stir for 1 minute, to coat the rice grains. Add the white wine, and cook until liquid is absorbed. Start adding the broth, a ladleful at a time, stirring continuously, until liquid has been absorbed. Continue adding broth a ladle at a time until broth is used up and rice is cooked.

4. Stir in mushrooms, grated lemon rind, cheese, and parsley, serve immediately.

Ingredients

2 tbsp/1 oz/25g butter

8 cups/1lb/500g mixed mushrooms (oyster,

shiitake, flat, enoki, portobello), sliced

2½ tbsp/40ml olive oil

2 cloves of garlic, minced

1 leek, finely sliced

1 quart/1¾ pints/1 chicken broth

Mixed Mushroom **Risotto**

2 cups/1 lb/450g Arborio (Italian) short-grain rice

½ cup/4fl oz/125ml dry white wine

1 lemon, rind finely grated

½ cup/4oz/125g pecorino cheese, grated

½ cup/4oz/125g Parmesan cheese, grated

2 tbsp/50g minced parsley

Italian

Method

1. Combine egg yolks and sugar in a heatproof bowl, and beat, until thick and pale. Beat in the sweet wine, and place the bowl over a saucepan of simmering water. Continue to beat for 15 minutes, or until the mixture is very thick, not allowing the bowl to overheat. The mixture will be ready when it forms soft mounds.

2. Remove the bowl from the heat, and continue beating for a further 5 minutes, or until the mixture has cooled. Fold in the passionfruit pulp, and serve with the fresh berries.

3. For Vanilla Zabaglione: Omit the passionfruit pulp and add seeds from 1 vanilla pod by splitting the pod down the center and scraping out the seeds.

Passionfruit Zabaglione with Fresh Berries

Ingredients

5 egg yolks

½ cup/4oz/125g caster (superfine) sugar

½ cup/4fl oz/125ml sweet white wine

5 tbsp/2½oz/85ml passionfruit pulp

½ cup/4oz/125g blueberries

⅔ cup/150g/5oz raspberries

⅔ cup/150g/5oz strawberries

Italian

Method

1. Preheat oven to 370°F/190°C.

2. Melt chocolate and butter over hot water, remove from heat, and stir in egg yolks, sugar, flour, nuts, and Frangelico liqueur. Beat egg whites until soft peaks form.

3. Fold lightly into chocolate mixture and pour into a greased and lined round, 8in/20cm cake pan, and bake for 40-45 minutes, or until cake shrinks slightly from sides of pan.

4. To make the Raspberry Sauce, place raspberries, powdered sugar and lemon juice in a food processor, and blend, until smooth. Strain, and add a little water if mixture is too thick.

5. Serve cake, cut into wedges, with raspberry sauce and cream.

Ingredients

6oz/200g dark chocolate, chopped

⅓ cup/3oz/100g butter

½ cup/60g/2 oz hazelnuts or pecans, ground

5 eggs, separated

½ cup/4 oz/125g caster sugar

⅓ cup/1½ oz/40g self-rising flour, sifted

3 tbsp/1½fl oz/50ml Frangelico liqueur

Frangelico Chocolate Cake with Raspberry Sauce

Sauce:

1 cup/250g/8oz raspberries

2 tbsp/30g powdered sugar

1 tbsp/15ml lemon juice

Italian

Method

1. Combine basil, sugar, and wine in a saucepan over medium heat. Bring to the boil. Cook, stirring, for 3 minutes.

2. Strain mixture. Discard solids. Cool to room temperature. Stir in lemon and lime juices and grated lemon rind.

3. Pour mixture into a shallow freezerproof container. Freeze until ice crystals start to form around the edges. Using a fork, stir to break up ice crystals. Repeat the process once more. Transfer mixture to ice cube trays. Freeze until firm.

Lemon and Basil Granita

Ingredients

2 tbsp/1oz/30g basil leaves, chopped

¼ cup/60g/2oz superfine (castor) sugar

2 cups/500ml/16fl oz sweet white wine

1 cup/250ml/8fl oz lemon juice

¼ cup/60ml/2fl oz lime juice

1 tbsp/15g grated lemon rind

Italian

Index